mingei: folk arts of old japan

mingei

folk arts of old japan

by Hugo Munsterberg

the asia society, inc. · distributed by harry n. abrams, inc.

MINGEI: FOLK ARTS OF OLD JAPAN is the catalogue
of an exhibition selected by Dr. Hugo Munsterberg
and shown in Asia House Gallery in the spring of 1965
as an activity of The Asia Society to further greater
understanding and mutual appreciation between the
United States and the peoples of Asia.

An Asia House Gallery Publication.

Copyright 1965 by The Asia Society, Inc.

Library of Congress Catalog Card Number: 65–19378

Contents

Foreword

"When shops have been opened to sell folk art," someone sadly remarked, "the end of folk art is already in sight." This wise observation points to the fact that the folk arts are the unself-conscious products of a people and are not made as merchandise in the modern sense of the term. Today, most of what is sold in the shops under this label is folk-artish in type rather than true folk art. It is no longer a rural craftwork made for family or neighborly consumption, but is rather a volume production of "hand-crafted gift ware" turned out to assuage our urban nostalgia for a lost world of country traditions and pleasures.

This exhibition of "Mingei: Folk Arts of Old Japan" looks back to a time before folk art was collected and long before it was produced for craft outlets in our cities. It offers us a glimpse of the anonymous art of Japan that was made in accordance with a way of life and traditions that have but little continuance today.

One of the tests of a definition of folk art must surely be its anonymity. Good craftsmanship must always have been appreciated, but the craftsman himself was not always name-known and ego-celebrated. Back of his work, or above it, there will sometimes have been court masters whose creations can be credited as his models. But it should also be claimed for the folk artist that at best, in a feudal society such as that of Japan, he transcended a mere imitation of court material. In other words, good folk art always had its own intrinsic values. Among these rustic virtues we will find great vigor, directness, and simplicity, as well as an engaging naiveté and a healthy, muscular roughness that sets it apart from the arts of the courts with their marvelous refinement, complexity, and elegance.

Folk art such as Japan's is thus seen to have been the work of unpolished country people, taking its strength from the land and requiring neither sophistication nor even a high degree of expertness in technique. What gives satisfaction is the simple poetry we find in it. Such art shares its freshness with the equally anonymous creations of nature herself, and may seem to have a similar kind of instinctive life beyond the intellect's appetite for analysis.

Not all students of the court arts of Japan have also enjoyed her folk arts. But it is of interest to note from the lenders' list in this catalogue that a number of specialists, among them the author Hugo Munsterberg, Usher P. Coolidge, Robert Treat Paine, Sherman Lee, and the late Langdon Warner and James Marshall Plumer, have included these arts in their affections. As ever, we are deeply grateful not only to our distinguished author, who also chose the material shown in our gallery, but to all others who have so kindly contributed to this exhibition.

Gordon Bailey Washburn, Director
Asia House Gallery

Lenders

Mr. and Mrs. James W. Alsdorf, Winnetka, Illinois

Mr. Joseph Breitenbach, New York City

Mr. Sidney B. Cardozo, New York City

The Cleveland Museum of Art, Cleveland, Ohio

Mr. and Mrs. Usher P. Coolidge, Cambridge, Massachusetts

Cooper Union Museum for the Arts of Decoration, New York City

The Detroit Institute of Arts, Detroit, Michigan

Dr. and Mrs. Robert Dickes, Brooklyn, New York

Mr. and Mrs. Myron S. Falk, Jr., New York City

Fogg Art Museum, Harvard University, Cambridge, Massachusetts

Mr. and Mrs. Charles Gadd, New York City

N. V. Hammer, Inc., New York City

Mr. Edwin Hewitt, Tokyo, Japan

Mr. Howard C. Hollis, New York City

Marion Jacob, Zurich, Switzerland

Japan Society, Inc., New York City

Mr. and Mrs. Samuel Josefowitz, New York City

Mathias Komor, New York City

Mrs. Mathias Komor, New York City

Mrs. Werner Koppitz, Mt. Kisco, New York

Dr. and Mrs. Sherman E. Lee, Cleveland, Ohio

Doris Meltzer, New York City

Dr. and Mrs. Hugo Munsterberg, New Paltz, New York

Museum of Art, The University of Michigan, Ann Arbor, Michigan

Mr. George K. Nakashima, New Hope, Pennsylvania

Prints Division, The New York Public Library, New York City

Spencer Collection, The New York Public Library, New York City

Mingei Kan, Tokyo, Japan

Mr. Douglas W. Overton, New York City

Mr. Robert T. Paine, Boston, Massachusetts

Mrs. James Marshall Plumer, Ann Arbor, Michigan

Mr. Langdon J. Plumer, Ledyard, Connecticut

Mr. and Mrs. John D. Rockefeller 3rd, New York City

Miss Beatrice G. Rothbard, Brooklyn, New York

Mr. Raymond Saroff, New York City

Seattle Art Museum, Seattle, Washington

The Author

Hugo Munsterberg was born in Berlin, Germany, on September 13, 1916. He came to America in 1935, and attended Harvard where he received his A.B. and Ph.D. degrees. He has taught at Wellesley College, Michigan State University, International Christian University in Tokyo, and Hunter College in New York.

Dr. Munsterberg lived in Japan from 1952 to 1956. At present he is Professor of Art History at the New York State University College at New Paltz. A collector of Japanese art, he has written numerous books and articles, among them *The Arts of Japan, The Folk Arts of Japan,* and *The Ceramic Art of Japan.*

*The circular crests on this and other pages throughout the book
are motifs taken from No. 89, Futon Cover (not illustrated).*

Chronology

The exhibition is comprised of folk
art created during the following periods
in the history of Japan:

Heian:	794–1185
Kamakura:	1185–1333
Muromachi:	1334–1573
Momoyama:	1573–1615
Early Edo:	1615–1703
Middle Edo:	1703–1800
Late Edo:	1800–1868

48. Detail from "The Procession of Rice-Pounding Dances at the Festival of Wakanoura."
Edo Period; early 19th c. Wakajama, near Osaka. 10 by 184 inches.

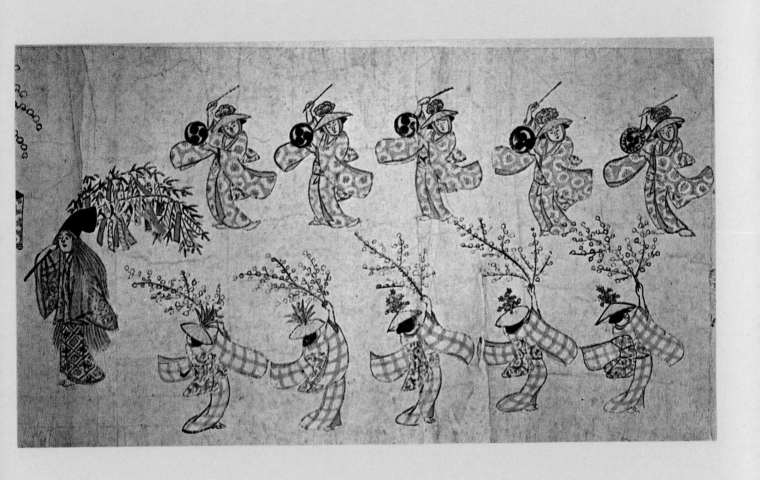

Introduction

If there is one quality which distinguishes Japanese art from the other great artistic traditions of Asia, it is the remarkable aesthetic sensibility which exists even among ordinary people and in every day life. While the greatest art of India is its religious sculpture, created under Buddhist and Hindu inspiration, and the supreme expressions of the Chinese artistic genius are the ink paintings which represent Taoist-inspired landscapes and which were primarily the product of a class of gentlemen-scholars, Japan's greatest contribution to the arts of the world is to be found in her crafts and domestic architecture. Here, among the rich and varied output of the craftsmen, some of the finest works of Japanese art are found. Names such as Kenzan and Korin in earlier times, and Rosanjin and Hamada in our own day, are as revered in Japan as are the names of Rembrandt and Picasso in the West. Among those whom the Emperor has designated as "living cultural treasures" of the Japanese nation, there are not only painters, sculptors, and architects, but also potters, weavers, dyers, lacquer manufacturers, and metal workers. In the eyes of the Japanese, a tea bowl or a textile can be as great a masterpiece as any work of the so-called fine arts, such as a painting or a sculpture.

Perhaps the most remarkable aspect of this outstanding production of crafts is the fact that activity was not restricted to the artist-craftsman working for the feudal aristocracy at the various courts, or employed by the rich merchants of the cities, but was universal, including small town artisans and traders as well as simple peasants. The Japanese term for this popular form of craft is *mingei,* or folk art, derived from the word *min,* meaning people or folk, and *gei,* meaning skills or arts. It is to these folk arts that the present exhibition is dedicated—arts which have a greater appeal to modern taste than the brightly colored porcelains which an older generation of Japan-enthusiasts so much admired.

The man chiefly responsible for the discovery of the special beauty of the folk art of Japan was the late Soetsu Yanagi. A prolific author and eloquent speaker, Dr. Yanagi devoted much of his life to furthering the appreciation of this art form. By founding the Japan Folk Art Society and establishing the Mingei Kan (Folk Art Museum) in Tokyo, he helped to encourage and support the folk arts, as well as to insure that the great treasures of the traditional *mingei* of Japan would be preserved for the Japanese nation. Lecturing at Harvard University in 1930, and publishing in English in 1936 a small but excellent introduction to Japanese folk art, Dr. Yanagi was able to share his enthusiasm with his American friends and help to make *mingei* known in the United States. He also brought to America the nucleus of a significant collection of Japanese folk art which is now owned by the Japan Society in New York, a part of which is on display in this exhibition.

Among the numerous friends and admirers of Soetsu Yanagi in America, the most important for the growth of appreciation of *mingei,* in this country were the late Langdon

Warner, for many years Curator of Oriental Art at the Fogg Museum and Lecturer at Harvard University, and his friend and former pupil, James Marshall Plumer, the late Professor of Oriental Art at the University of Michigan. Both shared their interest and enthusiasm for *mingei* with their many pupils, and saw to it that outstanding examples of Japanese folk art were displayed in the museums of this country. Both of them also collected *mingei* and, through the generosity of Mrs. Warner and Mrs. Plumer, it has been possible to include in this exhibition some of the works they collected.

While Yanagi, Warner, and Plumer were pioneers who had become interested in Japanese folk art before the Second World War, many others, both in Japan and the West, discovered the beauty of *mingei* in the post-war years. Indeed, there has occurred a veritable craze for Japanese folk works, with shops of contemporary *mingei* springing up in all major Japanese cities and department stores installing folk art sections. Through the interest of the many Americans who came to Japan during these years, either as soldiers or as part of the occupation personnel, *mingei* also became widely known and admired in America, and now has many collectors and enthusiasts in this country as well. Museums, too, notably the Seattle Art Museum under the leadership of Dr. Richard Fuller, began to collect Japanese folk art, and in 1958 with the support of the Japan Society the first complete study of Japanese folk art was published in English by the author (see Bibliography, p. 143).

The history of popular arts in Japan may be traced back to the later Heian period, that is, as far back as the tenth century, and we are fortunate in having in this exhibition an album of Buddhist folk prints from the Heian and Kamakura periods lent by the Spencer collection of the New York Public Library. No doubt many other types of *mingei* objects were made during these early centuries but most of them have perished as no effort was made to preserve them. However, the golden age of Japanese folk art did not arrive until the Edo period, 1615 to 1868, when, under the despotic but benevolent rule of the Tokugawa shoguns, the country enjoyed peace and prosperity. For the first time ordinary people, both in the villages and in small country towns, were able to enjoy a certain amount of leisure, and so could devote their skills to making objects which combined utility with beauty.

As Lincoln said of government, so one can also say of *mingei*—it was an art "of the people, by the people and for the people." Turned out by anonymous artisans in the provincial regions of the country, it was made without any thought of creating a work of art. It was a true folk production, unpretentious and simple, yet for that very reason often aesthetically outstanding. It existed side by side with the aristocratic art of the feudal courts and was often derived from the more sophisticated work of the cultural centers; it flourished in the peasant villages and small country towns right through the Edo period. Much of the output of these local craftsmen has undoubtedly been lost, but thanks to the efforts of Dr. Yanagi and other

19

mingei collectors, enough has been preserved from the Edo period to give a good picture of the many-sided and excellent craftsmanship which prevailed among the unknown and uncelebrated artists of the common people.

It would be difficult to list the many fields in which these folk artists were active, some of which, like the peasant architecture of rural Japan, unfortunately cannot be represented in this exhibition. Even though we cannot present the magnificent peasant house, a wealth of other material is at our disposal. Yet this selection of *mingei* objects from public and private collections in America can only suggest some of the areas in which these artists had their greatest success. Perhaps their most remarkable achievement was in ceramics, a craft which, therefore, is represented by the largest group of objects in this exhibition. Most of them are crude stoneware pieces designed for utilitarian purposes, such as the oil plates which were used under the traditional Japanese lamps to catch the dripping oil. Other types are the stoneware plates found in the kitchens of the peasant houses, sake bottles, water jars, and various containers for both liquids and foodstuffs. What they all have in common is a certain honesty and strength, suited to the environment for which they were intended.

Next to ceramics, textiles played the largest role in the life of the Japanese peasants. Kimonos with woven, dyed, or embroidered designs were produced throughout Japan, often showing great beauty of color, pattern, and texture. Painting and sculpture, the art forms most people think of when they talk of art today, had only a minor role. Outstanding among the former are the paintings made at Otsu which were sold as souvenirs to travelers on the Tokaido road, and usually represented popular deities or folk heroes. Another type is seen in the votive paintings, known as *Ema,* literally a "picture horse," dedicated to the Shinto shrines in lieu of the actual animal which was given in earlier times, although many subjects besides horses were portrayed. Among the sculptures, the stone carvings of popular deities are the most notable. While crude in execution they often have a freshness and naive charm which makes them very appealing. Far more important were the many objects made of wood, lacquer, and bamboo such as spoons, bowls, decanters, boxes, and containers of all types, as well as metal objects such as the hot water kettles made in Northern Japan. Outstanding among the works of this type are the typically Japanese *sumi-tsubo,* carpenters' reels used to make lines with an inked thread; the hooks, known as *jizai-kagi,* from which the kettles were suspended over the fires; and the marvelous wooden chests with metal decorations, called *tansu* in Japanese.

Although the production of *mingei* was not limited to any one region but was found in practically all districts of rural Japan, there were certain sections which excelled in one medium or the other. For example, the most impressive peasant houses were found in the village of Shirakawa in Gifu prefecture, huge, spacious buildings with large, overhanging roofs unique to this particular locality. Among the ceramic centers, the town of Seto not far from present day Nagoya was always outstanding. It was here that the celebrated oil drip plates, or *abura-zara*, and the stoneware plates, or *ishi-zara*, were manufactured. But Kyushu was equally important, for in Saga prefecture are located Arita, the center of porcelain manufacture, as well as Karatsu, in the neighborhood of which some of the finest folk ceramics were made. Other important kiln sites are found in the mountain villages of central Kyushu as well as in the region around Kagoshima, or Satsuma as it was once called, at the very Southernmost tip of the country.

Folk textiles have been produced all over Japan, but the finest were those made in Okinawa where the tribute to the local ruler was paid in cloth rather than rice, so that his subjects competed with each other to produce ever more beautiful kimonos. Another region in which a great variety of interesting textiles was made was Tohoku, the Northern portion of the main island of Honshu, where stencil-dyed and embroidered kimonos were outstanding. The finest woven designs, on the other hand, were found in the Tamba district in the mountain region north of Osaka, which was also well known for its ceramics.

Metal work was best in the Iwate and Yamagata regions of Northern Japan, while lacquer of the highest quality came from Kanazawa as well as Northern Shikoku, especially around Takamatsu. The finest bambooware is said to have been made in Kyushu and in the Western part of Shikoku, especially Kochi prefecture. The best known center for folk painting was the group of villages in the neighborhood of Otsu on Lake Biwa, while *Ema* were made all over Japan, but are perhaps most outstanding in the region around Kyoto and Nara. Folk sculptures are found everywhere in wayside shrines, but the most interesting are those from the region of Nara and the mountain villages of Nagano prefecture.

A list such as this is by no means exhaustive. Dozens of other localities could be mentioned which were outstanding in some field or other, as the excellence and variety of the rural arts are so great that new objects of beauty are continually discovered by folk art enthusiasts.

Probably all the works in this exhibition were made before the Meiji restoration in 1868 when Japan was opened up to the West. From that date, Western ideas and techniques began to come into the country, a development particularly detrimental to local handicrafts which thereafter had to compete with cheap, machine made objects produced in modern factories. But in the remote parts of Japan folk art has continued to flourish. Especially in the mountain villages of Kyushu and in the backward and poverty stricken villages of Tohoku, excellent *mingei* is still being produced, in contrast to the region around the great urban centers of Tokyo Nagoya, Kyoto, and Osaka where mass-produced, machine made objects have entirely replaced those made by rural craftsmen. Unfortunately, as the forces of modern Western civilization spread, and TV and washing machines reach the isolated villages, the beautiful stoneware dishes will be replaced by cheap bone china from Nagoya, and the sake bottles of old will disappear in an avalanche of plastic containers and beer cans.

Due to the efforts of Dr. Yanagi and other folk art enthusiasts an attempt is being made to keep the *mingei* tradition alive, and a large market for the products of these rural craftsmen has been developed in the urban centers of Japan and in the United States. All kinds of ceramics are being made, some of them genuine folk wares and others designed for modern use but derived from the folk art tradition. Hand woven cloth, handmade paper, beautiful metal objects as well as baskets of bamboo, vines, or grasses are still being produced in large quantities. Perhaps the most charming of the modern folk art objects are the numerous toys which are still being made in countless rural places all over Japan. A few examples of dolls of the Edo period are included in this exhibition, but literally hundreds of different folk toys of all types, some made of wood, others of *papier-mâché*, still others of clay or straw, are found all over the country. One of the most common types is the Daruma doll. These are believed to bring good luck to their owners, and it is said that former Prime Minister Ikeda, upon being asked to form a government by the Emperor, went home to draw eyes on his Daruma doll to thank it for bringing him such good fortune.

ceramics

and

lacquerware

24. *Shallow Bowl. Edo Period. Karatsu. Diam. 15⅞ inches.*

25. *Hizen Wine Bottle. Early Edo Period. Karatsu. H. 12 inches.*

3. Oil Drip Plate. Edo Period; 18th c.   Seto. Diam. 8¼ inches.

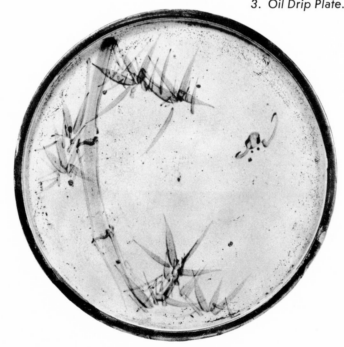

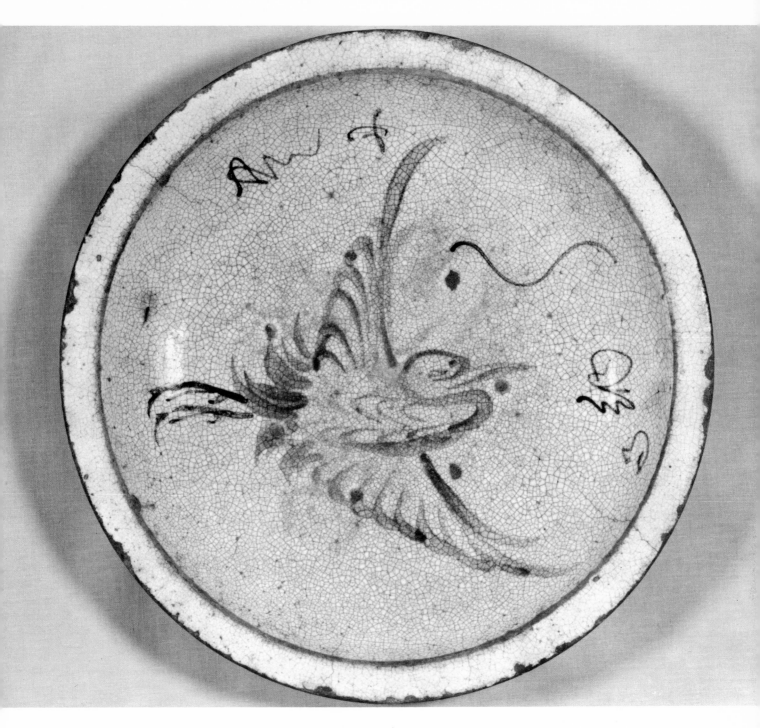

1. *Stone Ware Plate. Edo Period; 18th c.   Seto. Diam. 14 inches.*

2. *Oil Drip Plate. Edo Period; 18th c.   Seto. Diam. 10½ inches.*

27. Sake Bottle. Edo Period. Tamba. H. 8¼ inches.

5. Bottle. Edo Period; 18th c.   Tamba. H. 9¼ inches.

4. *Stone Ware Plate. Edo Period; 18th c. Seto. Diam. 11 inches.*

8. *Oil Drip Plate. Edo Period; 18th–19th c. Seto. Diam. 9¼ inches.*

15. Soba Cups. Two of a Set of Three. Edo Period; early 19th c.   Imari. Diam. 3⅛ inches, H. 2¼ inches.

29. Decanter. Edo Period. Diam. 7½ inches, H. 5⅜ inches.

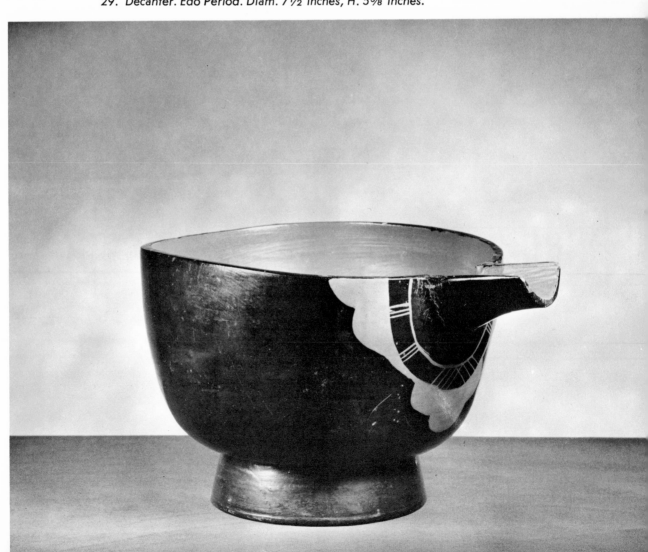

9. *Oil Drip Plate. Edo Period; 18th–19th c.   Seto. Diam. 9¾ inches.*

6. Stone Ware Bottle. Edo Period; 18th c.   Seto. H. 11¼ inches.

13. *Stone Ware Plate. Edo Period; early 19th c.   Seto. Diam. 8¼ inches.*

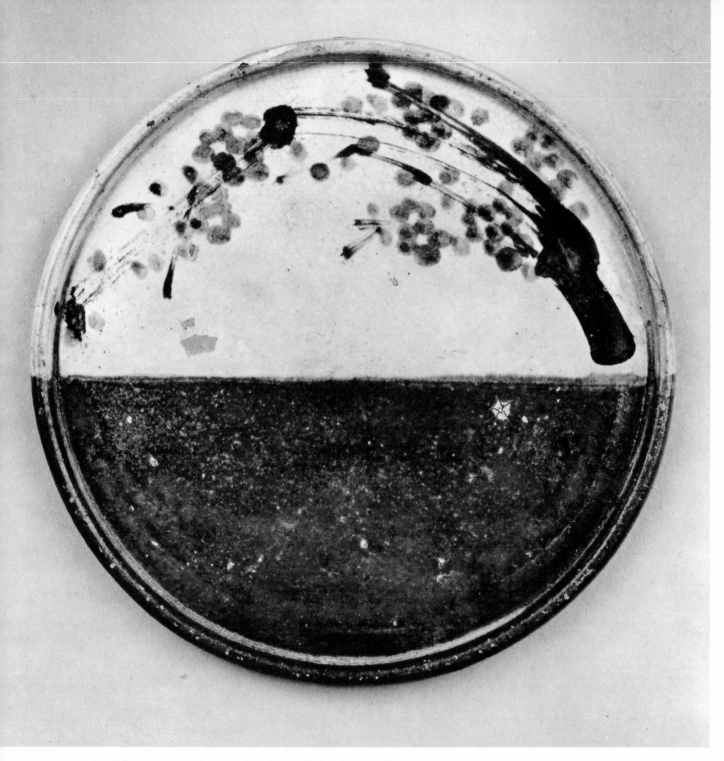

7. *Oil Drip Plate. Edo Period; c. 1800. Oribe. Diam. 8½ inches.*

14. *Bottle. Edo Period; early 19th c. Karatsu. H. 9⅝ inches.*

30. Container for Rice. Edo Period. Akiwa. Diam. 8¾ inches, H. 5¾ inches, H. of handle 13 inches.

31. Tea Jar. Edo Period. Diam. 2½ inches, H. 2¾ inches.

32. Plate. Edo Period. Takamatsu, Kagawa. Diam. 13¾ inches.

19. Oil Drip Plate. Edo Period. Seto. Diam. 11 inches.

28. Wine Bottle. Edo Period. Tamba. H. 8½ inches.

33. Water Bucket. Edo Period. Akita. Diam. 8¼ inches, H. 6 inches, H. of handle 12½ inches.

23. *Daikon Bowl. Edo Period. Tamba. Diam. 14½ inches (approx.), H. 7¼ inches.*

10. *Oil Drip Plate. Edo Period; 18th–19th c. Seto. Diam. 10½ inches.*

11. *Stone Ware Bowl. Edo Period; 1800. Diam. 4½ inches, H. 2⅜ inches.*

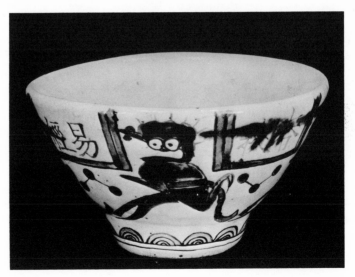

21. *Stone Ware Plate. Edo Period. Seto. Diam. 8¾ inches.*

26. *Bottle. Edo Period. Karatsu. H. 8⅛ inches.*

12. Stone Ware Plate. Edo Period; early 19th c. Seto. Diam. 9¼ inches.

18. Stone Ware Plate. Edo Period. Seto. Diam. 10½ inches.

34. Food Bowl. Edo Period; 19th c.   Hokkaido. Diam. 9⅜ inches, H. 6¾ inches.

35. Tea or Hot Water Pot. Edo Period; 19th c.   Hokkaido. Diam. 8¾ inches, H. 9¾ inches.

54

36. *Hidehira Bowl. Edo Period. Iwate. Diam. 4¾ inches, H. 3¼ inches.*

20. *Bowl. Edo Period. Seto. Diam. 7 inches, H. 3½ inches.*

paintings

and

sculptures

39. *Hunting Falcon, A Charm for a Good Harvest. Otsu-e.*
   Edo Period; late 17th or 18th c.   13 by 9½ inches.

51. *Acolyte of the Kasuga Shrine.*

Kamakura Period (1185–1392). H. 20 inches.

50. *Goddess.*

Attributed to Fugiwara Period (10th–12th c.). H. 38⅜ inches.

52. *Ebisu. Attributed to Ashikaga Period (1333–1573). H. 13¾ inches.*

37. *Votive Painting of a Horse. Ema. Edo Period; dated 1682. Signed: Hiroyuki. 21¾ by 33 inches.*

54. Monkey. Muromachi Period (1392–1568). H. 12½ inches.

38. Tametomo, a Famous Warrior of the Gempei Wars. Otsu-e.

Edo Period; late 17th or 18th c. 13 by 9½ inches.

53. Temple Horse. Ashikaga Period (1333–1573). Fukui. H. 25 inches.

63. Turtle. Edo Period; 19th c.   L. 3½ inches, W. 1¾ inches.

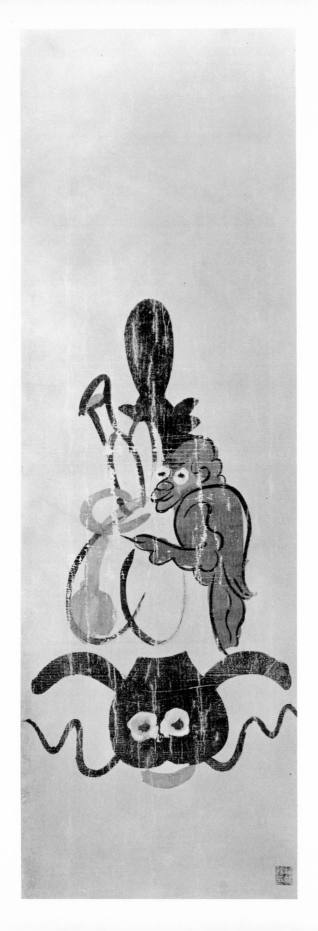

40. *Three of a Collection of Six Otsu-e.*

 All approximately 27⅜ by 9⅜ inches.

 c. *Naginata Benkei: The Strong Man*
  with Seven Weapons. Edo Period; early 18th c.

 a. *Kaminari to Taiko: The Thunder God Fishing His*
  Drum out of the Ocean. Edo Period; late 17th c.

 d. *Hyotan Namazu: The Monkey with Gourd*
  and the Catfish. Edo Period; early 18th c.

56. Fudo as God of the Underworld. Edo Period; 1800. H. 22 inches.

72

58. Sugawara-no-Michizane. Edo Period; mid-18th c.   H. 9 inches.

55. Enku Shonin Kannon. Edo Period; 17th c.   H. 20½ inches.

44. *Naginata Benkei: The Strongman. Otsu-e.*
Edo Period; 18th c.   24 by 9 inches.

41. *Fuji Musume: Wisteria Maiden.*
Otsu-e. Edo Period; early 18th c.
28 by 11⅜ inches.

61. *God. Edo Period; 18th c.   H. 15⅛ inches.*

62. *Fudo as God of the Underworld. Edo Period; 18th c.   H. 16½ inches.*

43. *Oni-no-Nembutsu:*

   The Devil Disguised as a Holy Man.

   Otsu-e. Edo Period; early 18th c.

   24 by 9½ inches.

49. *Oni-no-Nembutsu:*

The Devil Disguised as a Holy Man.

Otsu-e. Edo Period. 59 by 13⅞ inches.

60. Stag. Edo Period; 18th–19th c.   L. 33¾ inches.

46. Collection of Three Ema.

    c. *Praying Acolyte. Edo Period; 18th c.*
       4¼ by 6⅛ inches.

    a. *Horse. Edo Period; 18th c.*
       4⅛ by 5¼ inches.

    b. *Rooster and Hen. Edo Period; 18th c.*
       4¼ by 5⅝ inches.

59. Jizai-Kagi in the Shape of a Carp. Edo Period; 18th–19th c. L. 19½ inches.

57. Cat. Edo Period; 18th c.   H. 8¼ inches.

64. *Bird. Edo Period.*

H. 11 inches.

books

and

rubbings

65. "The Foot Print of the Buddha," from an album of thirty Buddhist prints.
Kamakura Period; 13th c.   12¼ by 5½ inches.

佛足石摺札　鎌倉中期刊

招提寺釋迦御舎利𬒈前不断之勤行光明真言二万遍　佛之千輻輪

釋迦如来荷持真言敬中下勃天御舎利供養末一斗可入御　長一尺捌寸

鉾給巴未来際之勤行僧伽盤桁巴

三千人之内供養末一手可被送招提寺藏入此衆人者雖一段小

二季彼戽奉讀三千佛名开過去現在名張可誦之矣可寄進之

66. Two pages from the book "The Princess in the Cave." Muromachi Period; dated 1540. 8¾ by 5⅝ inches (each page).

67. *Rubbing representing Village Gods. Edo Period; 17th c.   24⅜ by 21½ inches.*

68. *Rubbing representing Village Gods. Edo Period; 17th c. 25½ by 23 inches.*

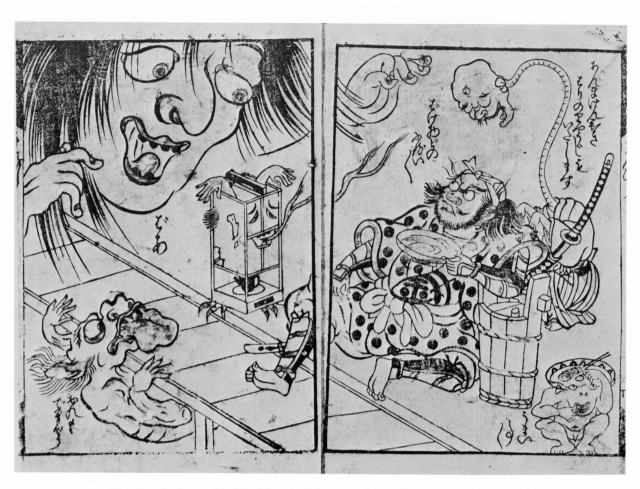

69. "Kinpira is not Afraid of Spooks," from the book "Kinpira and his Tour of Duty."
Edo Period; 1688. 7 by 5 inches (each page).

70. *Two pages from the book "Souvenir of Otsu." Edo Period; 1780. 14 by 10¼ inches (each page).*

71. *A page from the book "Dolls of Various Places." Edo Period; dated 1859. 10¾ by 7 inches.*

toys

75. Pair of Takeda Dolls. Edo Period. H. Man, 8 inches; Woman, 8¾ inches.

76. *Pair of Konosu Dolls. Edo Period. H. Man, 6¾ inches; Boy, 5⅞ inches.*

74. *Doll. Edo Period. Fushima. H. 5½ inches.*

73. Doll. Edo Period. Izukura. L. 11 inches.

72. Kite. Edo Period; 19th c.   56 by 35¼ inches.

textiles

78. Kimono. Edo Period; 18th c. Okinawa.

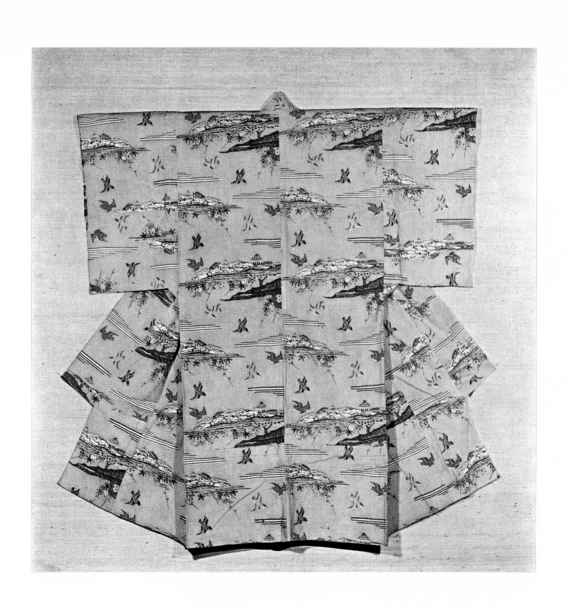

77. *Kimono. Edo Period; 18th c.   Okinawa.*

87. *Banner. Edo Period.*
    106 by 15½ inches.

81. *Katsugi. Edo Period. Tohoku.*

83. Kogin Embroidery. Edo Period. 32½ by 20¼ inches.

82. *Ainu Coat. Edo Period; 19th c. Hokkaido.*

85. *E-Kasuri Hanging. Edo Period.*
   33¾ by 12 inches.

84. *E-Kasuri Hanging. Edo Period.*
   29 by 13 inches.

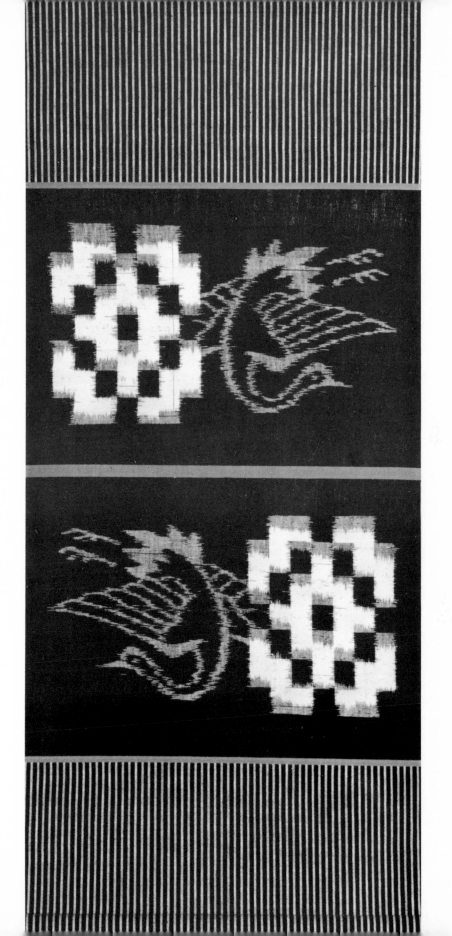

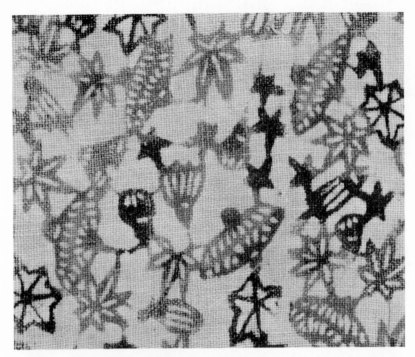

90b. *One of a Group of Four Dyed Textiles. Edo Period. Okinawa.*

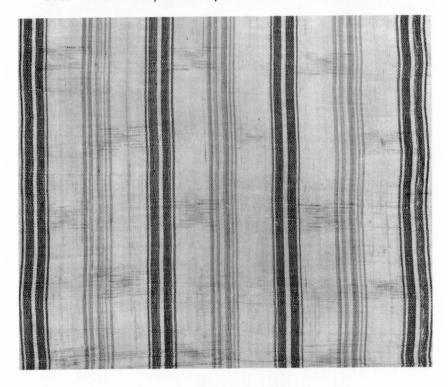

90a. *One of Two Woven Textiles. Edo Period. Okinawa.*

80. *Kimono. Edo Period; 18th c. Okinawa.*

90c. Dyed Textile. Edo Period. Okinawa.

88. Futon Cover. Edo Period. 60¾ by 48½ inches.

91f. One of a Group of Six Fabric Stencils.
Edo Period. 13¾ by 5¾ inches.

wood

and

metal

objects

92. Chest. Edo Period; 18th c.   H. 41⅜, W. 33½, D. 15⅜ inches.

99. Smoking Set. Edo Period. H. 11½, W. 8½, D. 8¼ inches.

97. *Hibachi. Edo Period. H. 11⅛, W. 9⅞, D. 8 inches.*

100. Bowl. Edo Period. H. 3½, Diam. 10¼ inches.

101. *Lantern. Edo Period. H. 10¾, Diam. 8 inches.*

93. Portable Candle Holder. Edo Period; 19th c. H. 3¾ inches.

98. Sea Chest. Edo Period; late 18th c. H. 24, W. 26½, D. 17⅜ inches.

94. Carpenter's Reel. Edo Period; 19th–20th c.   L. 10½ inches.

Catalogue*

Ceramics

1 Stone Ware Plate
Edo Period; eighteenth century. Seto.
Diam. 14 inches.
Flying crane design.
Museum of Art, The University of Michigan,
    Ann Arbor.

2 Oil Drip Plate
Edo Period; eighteenth century. Seto.
Diam. 10½ inches.
Blossom, *ha-na*, design.
Dr. and Mrs. Sherman E. Lee, Cleveland, Ohio.

3 Oil Drip Plate
Edo Period; eighteenth century. Seto.
Diam. 8¼ inches.
Bamboo design.
The Detroit Institute of Arts, Michigan.

4 Stone Ware Plate
Edo Period; eighteenth century. Seto.
Diam. 11 inches.
Crane design in iron glaze.
Mr. Robert T. Paine, Boston, Massachusetts.

*Objects not illustrated are marked with asterisks.

5 Bottle
Edo Period; eighteenth century. Tamba.
H. 9¼ inches.
Reddish brown with greenish brown drip-
    ping.
Dr. and Mrs. Hugo Munsterberg, New Paltz,
    New York.

6 Stone Ware Bottle
Edo Period; eighteenth century. Seto.
H. 11¼ inches.
Beige with black dripping.
Mr. Howard C. Hollis, New York City.

7 Oil Drip Plate
Edo Period; c. 1800. Oribe.
Diam. 8½ inches.
Plum design.
N. V. Hammer, Inc., New York City.

8 Oil Drip Plate
Edo Period; eighteenth–nineteenth century.
    Seto.
Diam. 9¼ inches.
Pine tree design.
Seattle Art Museum, Washington. Eugene
    Fuller Memorial Collection.

9 Oil Drip Plate

Edo Period; eighteenth–nineteenth century. Seto.

Diam. 9¾ inches.

Orchids and dragonfly design.

Seattle Art Museum, Washington. Eugene Fuller Memorial Collection.

10 Oil Drip Plate

Edo Period; eighteenth–nineteenth century. Seto.

Diam. 10½ inches.

Pine, bamboo, and plum blossom design.

Seattle Art Museum, Washington. Eugene Fuller Memorial Collection.

11 Stone Ware Bowl

Edo Period; 1800.

Diam. 4½ inches, H. 2⅜ inches.

Decorated with four *kappa,* or water imps.

Seattle Art Museum, Washington. Gift of Nasli Heeramaneck.

12 Stone Ware Plate

Edo Period; early nineteenth century. Seto.

Diam. 9¼ inches.

Rabbit and grass design.

Dr. and Mrs. Hugo Munsterberg, New Paltz, New York.

13 Stone Ware Plate

Edo Period; early nineteenth century. Seto.

Diam. 8¼ inches.

Horse-eye design.

Dr. and Mrs. Hugo Munsterberg, New Paltz, New York.

14 Bottle

Edo Period; early nineteenth century. Karatsu.

H. 9⅝ inches.

Dark brown and black with light grey neck.

Dr. and Mrs. Hugo Munsterberg, New Paltz, New York.

15 Soba Cups, Set of Three

Edo Period; early nineteenth century. Imari.

Diam. 3⅛ inches, H. 2¼ inches.

White with blue design.

Dr. and Mrs. Hugo Munsterberg, New Paltz, New York.

16 Tea Bowl*

Edo Period; early nineteenth century. Fujina.

Diam. 4 inches, H. 3 inches.

Celadon color glaze.

Dr. and Mrs. Hugo Munsterberg, New Paltz, New York.

17 Stone Ware Plate*

Edo Period. Seto.

Diam. 11 inches.

Willow and bird design.

N. V. Hammer, Inc., New York City.

18 Stone Ware Plate

Edo Period. Seto.

Diam. 10½ inches.

Grass, moon, and geese design.

N. V. Hammer, Inc., New York City.

19 Oil Drip Plate

Edo Period. Seto.

Diam. 11 inches.

Design representing the Zen concept of a broom sweeping away three basic human desires.

N. V. Hammer, Inc., New York City.

20 Bowl

Edo Period. Seto.

Diam. 7 inches, H. 3½ inches.

Beige ground with vine trellis design.

Marion Jacob, Zurich, Switzerland.

21 Stone Ware Plate

Edo Period. Seto.

Diam. 8¾ inches.

Tortoise and wave design.

Dr. and Mrs. Robert Dickes, Brooklyn, New York.

22 Oil Drip Plate*

Edo Period. Seto.

Diam. 7⅜ inches.

Bamboo design.

Dr. and Mrs. Robert Dickes, Brooklyn, New York.

23 Daikon Bowl

Edo Period. Tamba.

Diam. 14½ inches (approx.), H. 7¼ inches.

Terracotta bowl for grating radishes.

N. V. Hammer, Inc., New York City.

24 Shallow Bowl

Edo Period. Karatsu.

Diam. 15⅞ inches.

Bamboo and water design.

Anonymous loan. Formerly collection of Wasaburo Mizumachi.

25 Hizen Wine Bottle

Early Edo Period. Karatsu.

H. 12 inches.

Reed design, iron glaze.

N. V. Hammer, Inc., New York City.

26 Bottle

Edo Period. Karatsu.

H. 8⅛ inches.

Butterfly and autumn grass design.

N. V. Hammer, Inc., New York City.

27 Sake Bottle

Edo Period. Tamba.

H. 8¼ inches.

Shrimp design, overglazed enamel.

N. V. Hammer, Inc., New York City.

28 Wine Bottle

Edo Period. Tamba.

H. 8½ inches.

Reddish body, blue-black overglaze.

N. V. Hammer, Inc., New York City.

Lacquerware

29 Decanter
Edo Period.
Diam. 7½ inches, H. 5⅝ inches.
Black lacquer with gold design and red
    interior.
Japan Society, Inc., New York City.

30 Container for Rice
Edo Period. Akiwa.
Diam. 8¾ inches, H. 5¾ inches, H. of handle
    13 inches.
Red lacquer with brown bands.
Mr. and Mrs. Charles Gadd, New York City.

31 Tea Jar
Edo Period.
Diam. 2½ inches, H. 2¾ inches.
Brown lacquer with olive green, orange, light
    orange, cream, and black bands.
Marion Jacob, Zurich, Switzerland.

32 Plate
Edo Period. Takamatsu, Kagawa.
Diam. 13¾ inches.
Red, brown, and yellow lacquer.
Marion Jacob, Zurich, Switzerland.

33 Water Bucket
Edo Period. Akita.
Diam. 8¼ inches, H. 6 inches, H. of handle
    12½ inches.
Red lacquer with reddish brown decoration
    and black interior.
Marion Jacob, Zurich, Switzerland.

34 Food Bowl
Edo Period; nineteenth century. Hokkaido.
Diam. 9⅜ inches, H. 6¾ inches.
Black lacquer with sea shell design in color
    and gold.
Mrs. James Marshall Plumer, Ann Arbor,
    Michigan.

35 Tea or Hot Water Pot
Edo Period; nineteenth century. Hokkaido.
Diam. 8¾ inches, H. 9¾ inches.
Red lacquer with leaf spray and disk design
    in black on pot and cover.
Mrs. James Marshall Plumer, Ann Arbor,
    Michigan.

36 Hidehira Bowl
Edo Period. Iwate.
Diam. 4¾ inches, H. 3¼ inches.
Black lacquer with design of red and yellow
    flowers and gold geometric pattern.
Mrs. Werner Koppitz, Mt. Kisco, New York.

Paintings

37 Votive Painting of a Horse. Ema
Edo Period; dated 1682 ("Ninth Year of Empo
    Happy Day of May").
Signed: Hiroyuki.
21¾ by 33 inches.
Kiri wood; horse sculptured in low relief,
    painted black, white, and soft red.
Mr. and Mrs. James W. Alsdorf, Winnetka,
    Illinois.

38 Tametomo, a Famous Warrior of the Gempei Wars. Otsu-e

Edo Period; late seventeenth or eighteenth century.

13 by 9½ inches.

Ink and color on paper.

Seattle Art Museum, Washington. Eugene Fuller Memorial Collection.

39 Hunting Falcon, A Charm for a Good Harvest. Otsu-e

Edo Period; late seventeenth or eighteenth century.

13 by 9½ inches.

Ink and color on paper.

Seattle Art Museum, Washington. Eugene Fuller Memorial Collection.

40 Collection of Six Otsu-e

Edo Period; seventeenth and eighteenth centuries.

Painted in black and colors on paper.

All approximately 27⅜ by 9⅜ inches.

A. Kaminari to Taiko: The Thunder God Fishing his Drum out of the Ocean.

Late seventeenth century.

B. Yarimochi Yakko: The Faithful Retainer.

Early eighteenth century.

C. Naginata Benkei: The Strong Man with Seven Weapons.

Early eighteenth century.

D. Hyotan Namazu: The Monkey with Gourd and the Catfish.

Early eighteenth century.

E. Zato: The Blind Beggar with Barking Dog.

Eighteenth century.

F. Kasa Wakashu: Young Man with Straw Hat.

Eighteenth century.

Prints Division, The New York Public Library, New York City.

41 Fuji Musume: Wisteria Maiden. Otsu-e

Edo Period; early eighteenth century.

28 by 11⅜ inches.

Color on paper.

The Cleveland Museum of Art, Ohio. Anonymous gift.

42 Daitoku Shaving the Head of Fukurokuju, the God of Longevity. Otsu-e*

Edo Period; late seventeenth or eighteenth century.

13 by 9½ inches.

Ink and color on paper.

Seattle Art Museum, Washington. Eugene Fuller Memorial Collection.

43 Oni-no-Nembutsu: The Devil Disguised as a Holy Man. Otsu-e

Edo Period; early eighteenth century.

24 by 9½ inches.

Ink and color on paper.

Mr. and Mrs. Usher P. Coolidge, Cambridge, Massachusetts.

44 Naginata Benkei: The Strongman. Otsu-e
Edo Period; eighteenth century.
24 by 9 inches.
Ink and color on paper.
Museum of Art, The University of Michigan,
Ann Arbor.

**45 Oni-no-Nembutsu: The Devil Disguised as a
Holy Man. Otsu-e***
Edo Period; eighteenth century.
24 by 9¾ inches.
Ink and color on paper.
Museum of Art, The University of Michigan,
Ann Arbor.

46 Collection of Three Ema
Edo Period; eighteenth century.
Color on wood.
A. Horse. 4⅛ by 5¼ inches.
B. Rooster and Hen. 4¼ by 5⅝ inches.
C. Praying Acolyte. 4¼ by 6⅛ inches.
Mrs. Mathias Komor, New York City.

47 Child Bathing in Hot Water. Ema
Edo Period; eighteenth century.
4¼ by 5⅝ inches.
Color on wood.
Dr. and Mrs. Sherman E. Lee, Cleveland, Ohio.

**48 The Procession of Rice-Pounding Dances at the
Festival of Wakanoura**
Edo Period; early nineteenth century. Waka-
jama, near Osaka.
10 by 184 inches.
Manuscript on paper, in scroll form.
Spencer Collection, The New York Public Li-
brary, New York City.

**49 Oni-no-Nembutsu: The Devil Disguised as a
Holy Man. Otsu-e**
Edo Period.
59 by 13⅞ inches.
Ink and color on paper.
Mr. Joseph Breitenbach, New York City.

Sculpture

50 Goddess
Attributed to Fujiwara Period (tenth–twelfth
centuries).
H. 38⅝ inches.
Wood.
Collection of Mr. and Mrs. Samuel Josefowitz,
New York City.

51 Acolyte of the Kasuga Shrine
Kamakura Period (1185–1392).
H. 20 inches.
Wood.
Mathias Komor, New York City.

52 Ebisu
Attributed to Ashikaga Period (1333–1573).
H. 13¾ inches.
Wood.
Marion Jacob, Zurich, Switzerland.

53 Temple Horse
Ashikaga Period (1333–1573). Fukui.
H. 25 inches.
Wood.
Mr. Edwin Hewitt, Tokyo, Japan.

54 Monkey
Muromachi Period (1392–1568).
H. 12½ inches.
Wood.
Mr. Langdon J. Plumer, Ledyard, Connecticut.

55 Enku Shonin Kannon
Edo Period; seventeenth century.
H. 20½ inches.
Wood.
Mr. and Mrs. Usher P. Coolidge, Cambridge,
Massachusetts.

56 Fudo as God of the Underworld
Edo Period; 1800.
H. 22 inches.
Stone, with color.
Mr. and Mrs. Usher P. Coolidge, Cambridge,
Massachusetts.

57 Cat
Edo Period; eighteenth century.
H. 8¼ inches.
Wood, painted brown, with metal eyes.
Mr. and Mrs. John D. Rockefeller 3rd, New
York City.

58 Sugawara-no-Michizane
Edo Period; mid-eighteenth century.
H. 9 inches.
Wood figure of the great Chinese scholar of
the eleventh century.
Seattle Art Museum, Washington. Eugene
Fuller Memorial Collection.

59 Jizai-Kagi in the Shape of a Carp
Edo Period; eighteenth–nineteenth century.
L. 19½ inches.
Wood carp with metal eyes, and iron hook.
(For suspending teakettle over fire.)
Seattle Art Museum, Washington. Eugene
Fuller Memorial Collection.

60 Stag
Edo Period; eighteenth–nineteenth century.
L. 33¾ inches.
Wood with actual deer's antlers.
Seattle Art Museum, Washington. Eugene
Fuller Memorial Collection.

61 God
Edo Period; eighteenth century.
H. 15⅛ inches.
Stone.
Susanno O (Horse God) or Gizu Tenno (Ox
God); wayside figure from the Island of
Sado.
Mr. Sidney B. Cardozo, New York City.

62 Fudo as God of the Underworld
Edo Period; eighteenth century.
H. 16½ inches.
Stone.
Wayside figure from the Island of Sado.
Mr. Sidney B. Cardozo, New York City.

63 Turtle

Edo Period; nineteenth century.

L. 3½ inches, W. 1¾ inches.

Wood.

Fogg Art Museum, Harvard University, Cambridge, Massachusetts, on loan from Mrs. Langdon Warner.

64 Bird

Edo Period.

H. 11 inches.

Wood.

Mr. and Mrs. Myron S. Falk, Jr., New York City.

Books and Rubbings

65 The Foot Print of the Buddha

Kamakura Period; thirteenth century.

12¼ by 5½ inches (print only).

From an album of thirty Buddhist prints from the Toshodai-ji at Nara.

Prints Division, The New York Public Library, New York City.

66 The Princess in the Cave

Muromachi Period; dated 1540.

8¾ by 5⅝ inches (each page).

Manuscript on paper, in book form; two volumes with seventy full-page watercolor drawings.

Spencer Collection, The New York Public Library, New York City.

67 Rubbing Representing Village Gods

Edo Period; seventeenth century.

Taken from a Nagano region stone carving.

24⅜ by 21½ inches.

Doris Meltzer, New York City.

68 Rubbing Representing Village Gods

Edo Period; seventeenth century.

Taken from a Nagano region stone carving.

25½ by 23 inches.

Doris Meltzer, New York City.

69 Kinpira is not Afraid of Spooks

Edo Period; 1688.

7 by 5 inches (each page).

From *Kinpira and his Tour of Duty*, a children's book with six woodcuts lightly colored by hand.

Spencer Collection, The New York Public Library, New York City.

70 Souvenir of Otsu

Edo Period; 1780.

14 by 10¼ inches (each page).

Book of colored woodcuts, with comic verses.

Spencer Collection, The New York Public Library, New York City.

71 Dolls of Various Places

Edo Period; dated 1859.

10¾ by 7 inches (each page).

Manuscript in book form with text and watercolor drawings by Toha Hikosaka.

Spencer Collection, The New York Public Library, New York City.

Toys

72 Kite
Edo Period; nineteenth century.
56 by 35¼ inches.
Silk on paper, with lacquered bamboo struts.
  Painted with a representation of Goeman
  Ishikawa, a thieves' boss.
Mr. Sidney B. Cardozo, New York City.

73 Doll
Edo Period. Izukura.
L. 11 inches.
Wood, colored white.
Mr. Raymond Saroff, New York City.

74 Doll
Edo Period. Fushima.
H. 5½ inches.
Plaster, painted.
Beatrice G. Rothbard, Brooklyn, New York.

75 Pair of Takeda Dolls
Edo Period.
H. Man, 8 inches; Woman, 8¾ inches.
Wood, lacquered, and cloth.
Japan Society, Inc., New York City.

76 Pair of Konosu Dolls
Edo Period.
H. Man, 6¾ inches; Boy, 5⅞ inches.
Wood, paper, and cloth, painted and lac-
  quered.
Japan Society, Inc., New York City.

Textiles

77 Kimono
Edo Period; eighteenth century. Okinawa.
Linen with "Bingata" (stencil-dyed) design.
Mingei Kan, Tokyo, Japan.

78 Kimono
Edo Period; eighteenth century. Okinawa.
Cotton with "Bingata" design.
Mingei Kan, Tokyo, Japan.

79 Kimono*
Edo Period; eighteenth century. Okinawa.
Banana plant fiber woven in polychrome
  "Kasuri" design.
Mingei Kan, Tokyo, Japan.

80 Kimono
Edo Period; eighteenth century. Okinawa.
Silk woven in "Tejima" design (plaid com-
  bined with "Kasuri" design).
Mingei Kan, Tokyo, Japan.

81 Katsugi
Edo Period. Tohoku.
Cotton, dyed blue and green.
Japan Society, Inc., New York City.

82 Ainu Coat
Edo Period; nineteenth century. Hokkaido.
Elm bark fiber with appliqué of cotton and
  embroidery.
Cooper Union Museum for the Arts of Deco-
  ration, New York City. Gift of Alice Boney.

83 Kogin Embroidery
Edo Period.
32½ by 20¼ inches.
Blue hemp fiber with white cotton embroidery.
Japan Society, Inc., New York City.

84 E-Kasuri Hanging
Edo Period.
29 by 13 inches.
Indigo and white cotton, woven design.
Marion Jacob, Zurich, Switzerland.

85 E-Kasuri Hanging
Edo Period.
33¾ by 12 inches.
Indigo and white cotton, woven design.
Marion Jacob, Zurich, Switzerland.

86 Banner*
Edo Period.
98 by 12½ inches.
Dyed and painted cloth, indigo, white, and persimmon, with family crest and characters "Hiro" (wide or spacious) and "Ta" (paddy field).
Marion Jacob, Zurich, Switzerland.

87 Banner
Edo Period.
106 by 15½ inches.
Hemp fiber painted with tiger design and family crest.
Japan Society, Inc., New York City.

88 Futon Cover
Edo Period.
60¾ by 48½ inches.
Cotton "mattress" cover with dyed paulownia and phoenix design.
Japan Society, Inc., New York City.

89 Futon Cover
Edo Period.
54½ by 50 inches.
Cotton "mattress" cover with dyed design of circular crests.
Japan Society, Inc., New York City.

90 Group of Okinawan Textile Fragments
Edo Period.
A. Two woven textiles.
B. Four dyed textiles.
C. One dyed textile.
D. Seven woven textiles.*
Dr. and Mrs. Hugo Munsterberg, New Paltz, New York.

91 Group of Six Fabric Stencils
Edo Period.
A: 13½ by 8 inches.*
B: 14½ by 6½ inches.*
C: 14 by 6½ inches.*
D: 13¾ by 8½ inches.*
E: 14⅝ by 7½ inches.*
Cut-out paper.
F: 13¾ by 5¾ inches.
Cut-out paper mounted on human hair.
Japan Society, Inc., New York City.

Wood and Metal Objects

92 Chest
Edo Period; eighteenth century.
H. 41⅜, W. 33½, D. 15⅜ inches.
Wood with metal fittings.
Mr. Douglas W. Overton, New York City.

93 Portable Candle Holder
Edo Period; nineteenth century.
H. 3¾ inches.
Iron with bronze decoration.
Anonymous loan.

94 Carpenter's Reel
Edo Period; nineteenth–twentieth century.
L. 10½ inches.
Wood and metal.
Fogg Art Museum, Harvard University,
    Cambridge, Massachusetts, on loan from
    Mrs. Langdon Warner.

95 Carpenter's Reel*
Edo Period.
L. 9 inches (approx.)
Wood and metal.
Mr. George K. Nakashima, New Hope, Pennsylvania.

96 Carpenter's Reel*
Edo Period.
L. 9 inches (approx.)
Wood and metal.
Mr. George K. Nakashima, New Hope, Pennsylvania.

97 Hibachi
Edo Period.
H. 11⅛, W. 9⅞, D. 8 inches.
Wood and metal.
Mr. Sidney B. Cardozo, New York City.

98 Sea Chest
Edo Period; late eighteenth century.
H. 24, W. 26½, D. 17⅜ inches.
Paulownia wood with iron fittings.
Mr. Sidney B. Cardozo, New York City.

99 Smoking Set
Edo Period.
H. 11½, W. 8½, D. 8¼ inches.
Paulownia wood with bronze fittings.
Mr. Sidney B. Cardozo, New York City.

100 Bowl
Edo Period.
H. 3½, Diam. 10¼ inches.
Iron with dark red lacquered cover.
Marion Jacob, Zurich, Switzerland.

101 Lantern
Edo Period.
H. 10¾, Diam. 8 inches.
Iron.
Anonymous loan.

102 Shop Sign*
   Edo Period.
   L. 15½, W. 9¼ inches.
   Wood and iron.
   Anonymous loan.

103 Jizai-Kagi*
   Edo Period.
   L. 58¼ inches.
   Iron.
   N. V. Hammer, Inc., New York City.

47. Child Bathing in Hot Water. Ema. Edo Period; 18th c. 4¼ by 5⅝ inches.

Bibliography

The Folk Art of Japan. Santa Fe, New Mexico; Museum of International Folk Art, 1958.

Fuller, Richard E. *Japanese Art in the Seattle Art Museum*. Seattle, 1960.

Hayashi, T. *Japanese Women's Folk Costumes*. Tokyo, 1960.

Kup, Karl. *Otsu-e of the Tokugawa Period, Print No. 10*. New York, 1956.

Munsterberg, Hugo. *The Ceramic Art of Japan*. Tokyo and Rutland, Vermont, 1964.

———————— *The Folk Arts of Japan*. Tokyo and Rutland, Vermont, 1958.

———————— "Japanese Folk Art in the Seattle Art Museum." *Oriental Art*, vol. VIII, 2, 1962.

Tanaka, Toshio. *Ishizara and Aburazara*. Kyoto, 1960.

Tanaka, Toshio and Reiko. *A Study of Okinawa Textile Fabrics*. Tokyo, 1952.

Warner, Langdon. *The Enduring Art of Japan*. Cambridge, Massachusetts, 1952.

Yamanaka, Sadajirō. "Japanese Pottery Oil Dishes." *Eastern Art*, vol. I, 1928.

Yanagi, Soetsu. *Folk Crafts of Japan*. Tokyo, 1936.

——————— "Folk Craft." *Contemporary Japan*, vol. VI, 3, 1937.

——————— *Illustrated Cyclopedia of Folk Crafts*, vols. I, II. Tokyo, 1960.

——————— "Japanese Rural Pottery." *Japan Quarterly*, vol. II, 1955.

——————— "A Note on Ishizara." *Eastern Art*, vol. III, 1931.

——————— "The Peasant Paintings of Otsu, Japan." *Eastern Art*, vol. II, 1930.